EXETER TO BARNSTAPLE

Vic Mitchell and Keith Smith

MP Middleton Press

First published May 1993

ISBN 1 873793 15 4

© Middleton Press 1993

Design - Deborah Goodridge
Typesetting - Barbara Mitchell

Published by Middleton Press
        Easebourne Lane
        Midhurst
        West Sussex
        GU29 9AZ
        Tel: (0730) 813169
(From 16 April 1995 - (01730) 813169)

Printed & bound by Biddles Ltd,
        Guildford and Kings Lynn

INDEX

ACKNOWLEGEMENTS

We have received considerable help from many of those mentioned in the photographic credits. We are very grateful for this and for the assistance given by R.M.Casserley, Dr.E.Course, G.Croughton, D.Dornom, N.W.Hearn, F.Hornby, P.Horne, M.King, N.Langridge, A.Ll.Lambert, Mr.D.&Dr.S. Salter, N.Stanyon, M.Turvey, A.E.West, E.Youldon and for the great help from our wives.

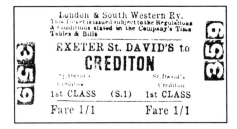

1955 map

- ━ Southern Region
- — Western Region
- ═ Former Lynton & Barnstaple Rly

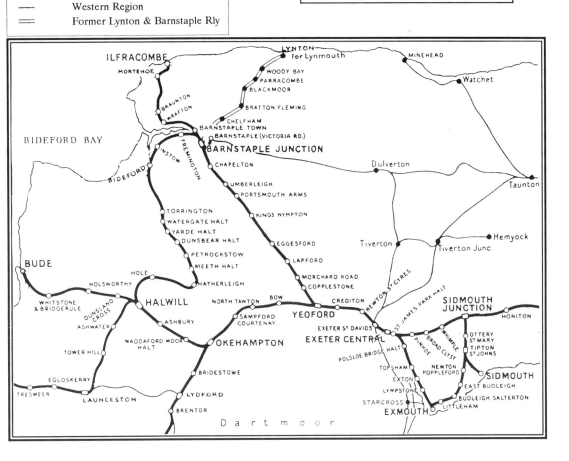

GEOGRAPHICAL SETTING

From the county town and cathedral city of Exeter, the route runs north in the narrow valley of the River Exe for over a mile. From Cowley Bridge Junction it follows the River Yeo and climbs steadily for nearly ten miles before leaving its valley near Yeoford. A further three miles takes the line to its summit near Copplestone, 350ft above sea level.

The 25 mile descent to Barnstaple involves running alongside another River Yeo in the vicinity of Lapford but this valley joins that of the River Taw about one mile north of that station. The Taw is followed closely for the remainder of the journey to Barnstaple, its presence necessitating several substantial bridges.

The geological structures of the area are of little economic importance, being mainly Millstone Grit and Culm Measures.

All maps are to the scale of 25" to 1 mile.

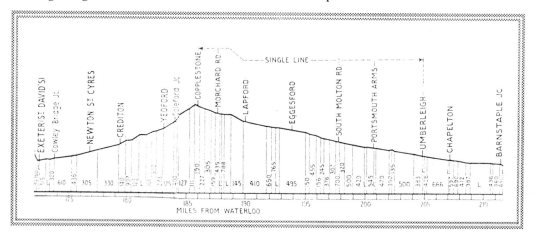

HISTORICAL BACKGROUND

The broad gauge Bristol & Exeter Railway was completed to Exeter on 1st May 1844. It was worked by the Great Western Railway until 1st May 1849 after which date operation was undertaken by the B&ER. The GWR purchased the route on 1st August 1876.

The route south to Teignmouth was opened by the South Devon Railway on 20th May 1846 and was later operated briefly on the atmospheric system. It was worked by the GWR from 1st February 1876 and absorbed by that company on 1st August 1878.

The London & South Western Railway's route from Yeovil to Exeter Queen Street (now Central) opened in 1860 and was extended to St. Davids on 1st February 1862. This was laid to standard gauge.

The Exeter & Crediton Railway's successful Act was passed on 21st July 1845. After protracted arguments the E&CR was leased to the B&ER and opened on 12th May 1851, having been ready for traffic since January 1847.

The Taw Vale Railway was opened between Barnstaple and Fremington for horse-drawn mineral traffic on 25th April 1848 and for broad gauge passenger services on 1st August 1854. On the same day the Crediton to Barnstaple section came into use, extension to Bideford following in 1855.

The LSWR already had shares in the Taw Vale Railway but was not able to lease the line until 1862.

The TVR along with the Crediton to Barnstaple section was known collectively as the North Devon Railway. Broad gauge trains between Exeter and Bideford were operated by the NDR itself from 28th July 1855.

From 1st February 1862, the LSWR leased the E&CR and soon added a third rail for its standard gauge trains to enable them to run through from Waterloo. These were extended from Crediton to Bideford on 2nd March 1863. Broad gauge goods trains continued to run to Barnstaple until 1877 and to Crediton until 1892. The GWR retained the right to operate freight trains to Crediton until 1903.

The LSWR reached Plymouth in 1876, the first section from Coleford Junction to North Tawton opening on 1st November 1865.

The Barnstaple Junction - Ilfracombe route was in use from 1874 until 1970 and the Taunton-Barnstaple line from 1873 until 1966, with trains diverted from 1960 from Victoria Road to Barnstaple Junction when Victoria Road was closed to passengers.

The connection between Barnstaple Junction and Barnstaple Victoria Road was open to traffic from 1887 until 1970, latterly only for goods. The Barnstaple-Fremington-Torrington route closed to passengers on 4th October 1965. Passenger trains continued to run to Okehampton until 5th January 1972. China clay traffic through Torrington and Bideford continued until 1982.

Doubling of the route north of Crediton commenced in 1879 but in 1910 an agreement was made between the LSWR and the GWR for the pooling of receipts for all competitive traffic. Thus the need to improve the route no longer existed and the Copplestone-Umberleigh section remained single.

The LSWR became part of the Southern Railway in 1923 and this in turn became the Southern Region of British Railways in 1948. In January 1963, Southern Region lines in Devon were transferred to the Western Region.

The stations opened with the line, unless otherwise stated.

PASSENGER SERVICES

The table below gives an indication of summer down train frequency and excludes services operating on less than five days per week.

	Weekdays		Sundays	
	Stopping	Express	Stopping	Express
1851	7	-	4	-
1855	5	-	2	-
1869	6	-	2	-
1890	6	1	1	1
1906	5	3	1	-
1914	6	2	1	1
1924	6	4	-	-
1934	8	2	2	2
1944	7	1	2	1
1954	8	1	4	1
1963	8	1	5	-
1965	8	-	6	-
1975	9	-	3	-
1980	7	-	3	-
1981	10	-	4	-
1992	9	-	3	-

There were one or two short workings between Exeter and Crediton shown in some timetables of the 1870-90 period. Four such trains were reintroduced in May 1992. Another long standing short working in the down direction was at about 8.20am from South Molton Road (Kings Nympton) to Barnstaple, operating for over 20 years up to 1964. Until that time all services ran through to Exeter Central or beyond, but thereafter most terminated at St. Davids. More recently an increasing number have reverted to Central. In 1992 all except two used Central and four terminated at Exmouth.

The "Atlantic Coast Express" and other weekday through trains from Waterloo ceased on 5th September 1964. The Brighton-Plymouth service continued to use the southern part of the route until 4th March 1967. Some summer Saturday through trains continued to operate, notably to and from Paddington until 1981 and to Waterloo until 1982.

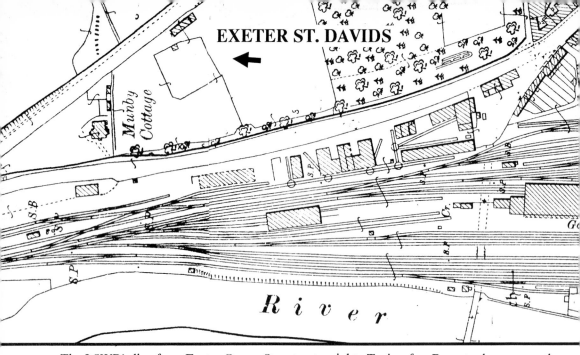

EXETER ST. DAVIDS

←

Munby Cottage

R i v e r

The LSWR's line from Exeter Queen Street is top right on this 1905 edition and the GWR's Taunton to Newton Abbot route runs from left to right. Trains for Barnstaple run on the Taunton line for over one mile to Cowley Bridge Junction.

1. Exeter's first station had two platforms, both on the down side and with crossovers between them. The arrangement was like the single through platform at Cambridge in use to this day. Work on this ornate structure started in 1860; five through platforms and 26 decorative urns were provided. The tracks of the electric tramway, which operated from 1905 to 1931, are marked on the map. (Lens of Sutton)

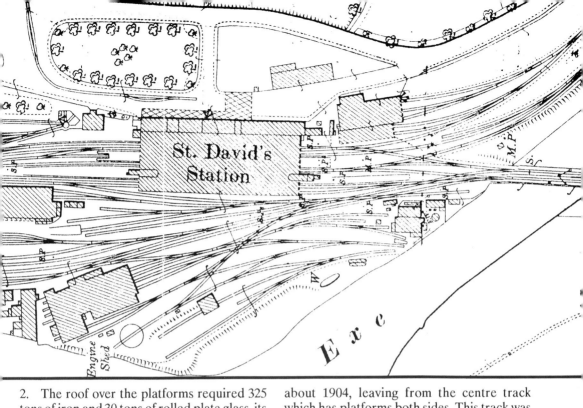

2. The roof over the platforms required 325 tons of iron and 30 tons of rolled plate glass, its maximum height being 60ft. An LSWR class C8 4-4-0 waits to depart north for Padstow in about 1904, leaving from the centre track which has platforms both sides. This track was the LSWR down line and the GWR's up. (R.S.Carpenter coll.)

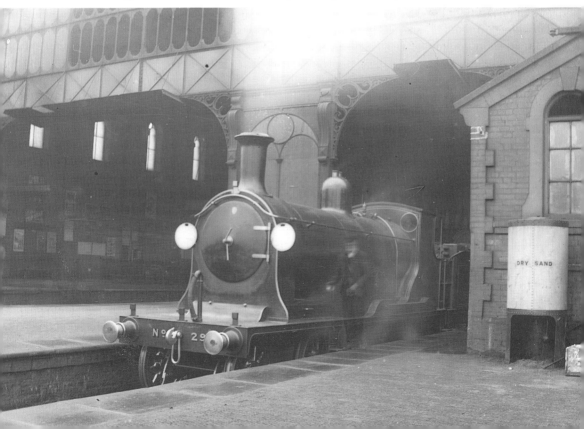

3. With the leading wagon endorsed "Transfer" (probably to the GWR Yard), class 380 4-4-0 no.383 blows off having come down the 1 in 37 from Exeter Queen Street. Hay, straw and manure comprised a large part of railway traffic in the pre-motor age. (R.S.Carpenter coll.)

4. In 1912 work started on the removal of the massive overall roof and the provision of individual platform canopies. This photograph from the late 1930s shows that the facade, offices and urns were retained. Class U1 no.1894 heads an up train, next stop Exeter Central which was named "Queen Street" until 1933. (Lens of Sutton)

5. Recorded on 25th May 1929, class T9 4-4-0 no.724 descends the incline from Queen Street in the company of class G6 0-6-0s nos. 237 and 257. These two banking engines had probably been attached to the train as a convenient way of working them between the two stations without special line occupation on a busy day. West Box is on the right and a GWR gas cylinder wagon is on the left. (H.C.Casserley)

6. A southward view shows that the 1912-13 rearrangement gave one through line, on which a tank wagon is standing. The line with two platforms was eliminated at this time, resulting in six through lines, five through platforms and one bay, visible on the left. Various additions were made in 1938, these including longer canopies. (Lens of Sutton)

8. No.34004 *Yeovil* waits to depart from platform 3 on 17th August 1953 with a train loaded with holidaymakers mostly destined for Waterloo. Note the inspection pit at platform 1. This was of value to drivers requiring to inspect the inside motion of GWR four-cylindered engines. (N.L.Browne)

7. A northward view has the bay (numbered 2) in the right distance and platform 1 on the right. Until 1985 this was used by trains bound for the Newton Abbot line and by some down trains terminating at St. Davids. There was much flexibility in platform working. (Lens of Sutton)

9. A Western Region train *from* London stands alongside a Southern Region train *to* London, separated by the through line usable by either non-stop or freight services. The line on the right serves the carriage sheds. The former GWR engine shed can be seen on the left. (Lens of Sutton)

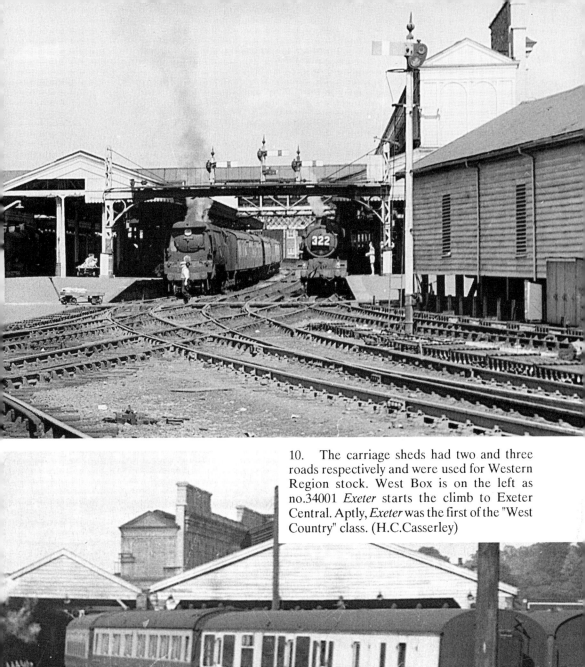

10.   The carriage sheds had two and three roads respectively and were used for Western Region stock. West Box is on the left as no.34001 *Exeter* starts the climb to Exeter Central. Aptly, *Exeter* was the first of the "West Country" class. (H.C.Casserley)

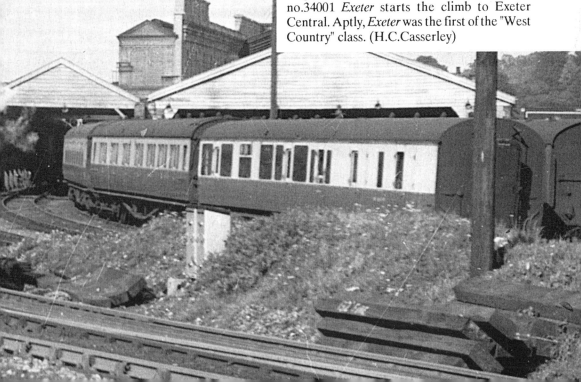

Exeter Central is illustrated and described in the companion albums *Yeovil to Exeter* and *Branch Lines around Exmouth*.

11. Until the advent of Bulleid Pacifics and diesels, many up trains required banking assistance to Exeter Central. Class E1/R nos.32135 and 32124 run towards an up stone train on 22nd May 1957. The Z class 0-8-0Ts undertook this work from 1959 to 1962, when class W 2-6-4Ts took over. (T.Wright)

12. At the north end of the platforms a level crossing adds to the operating difficulties of this complex junction. No.34032 *Camelford* arrives with a train for Waterloo on 14th September 1959. The other engine is on a short stub siding in front of Middle Box. This siding was the resting place for banking engines. (J.Scrace)

13.   On Saturdays, in the summer of 1982, alternate trains from Barnstaple were DMUs and locomotive hauled MkI coaches. No. 311407 heads an example of the latter on 14th August 1982. The last through working to Waterloo was the 08.25 from Barnstaple on 2nd October 1982, this train having run on Saturdays only that summer. (J.S.Petley)

14.   A DMU from Barnstaple is seen from Middle Box on 3rd December 1983. All the signal boxes in the Exeter area were replaced by a panel controlling colour light signals in April and May of 1985. (P.G.Barnes)

15. Centre is no.33027 with a ballast train on 30th May 1984. It is flanked by no.37307 with a freight, and parcel vans in the bay. Subsequently these two services have been decimated by the Government's mismanagement of transport policy and failure to pay for the environmental benefits of rail transport. (J.Scrace)

16. Since 1985 the down line from Exeter Central and all the platform lines have been signalled for reversible running. The through line between platforms 1 and 3 was removed at that time. No. P957 is working one of the increasing number of Barnstaple-Exmouth services. (Lens of Sutton)

NORTH OF EXETER

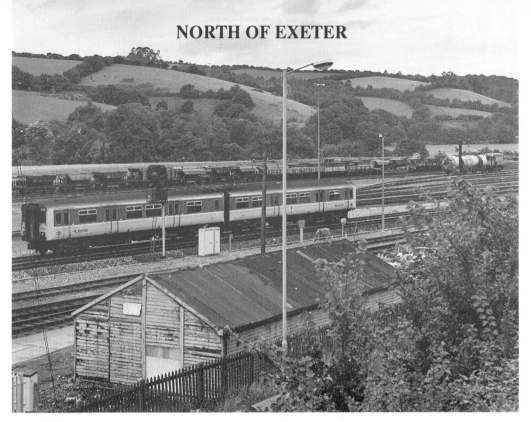

17. North of St. Davids, the Riverside Yard receives most of the few remaining freight services from the West of England. A class 150 Sprinter unit is working the 10.25 Exmouth to Barnstaple service on 24th August 1992. (D.Wilson).

COWLEY BRIDGE JUNCTION

19. The driver of the 10.38 from Barnstaple is ready to hand over the tablet to the signalman on 25th February 1985. The line from here to Newton St.Cyres had been doubled on 23rd February 1875. The part over the bridges had been singled during repairs in 1965 and permanently from 15th January 1967. The LSWR had its own signal box (near the rear of the train) from the 1880s until 1916. This ex-GWR box closed on 30th March 1985, the signals dating from 1943 when Riverside Yard was extended, as was the signal box. The name-plate remained in the centre of the original part of the box. (D.Mitchell)

18. The Western Region main line to London is on the right as class N no.31841 leaves the North Devon line with a stone train on 18th June 1957. The brake van is on the bridge over the River Exe, the cause of flooding of the junction on occasions. Immediately behind the photographer are the points of Riverside Yard. (E.W.Fry)

Newton St. Cyres	1928	1936
No. of passenger tickets issued	10385	5608
No. of season tickets issued	33	18
No. of tickets collected	10987	5683
No. of telegrams	394	23
Parcels forwarded	266	182
Parcels received	448	527
Horses forwarded	1	8
Milk forwarded	-	-
Milk received	-	-
General goods forwarded (tons)	466	128
General goods received (tons)	568	930
Coal, Coke etc.	272	237
Other minerals forwarded	-	-
Other minerals received	2099	578
Trucks livestock forwarded	10	38
Trucks livestock received	15	7
Lavatory pennies	-	48

20. The station opened as "St.Cyres" and was renamed on 1st October 1913. The line on to Crediton was doubled on 2nd June 1875 and the broad gauge rails were removed in 1892. (Lens of Sutton)

The 1905 map shows the isolated position of the station. It is nearly one mile north of the village, whose population fell from 960 to 830 in the 100 years from 1871. The position of the signal box is marked SB.

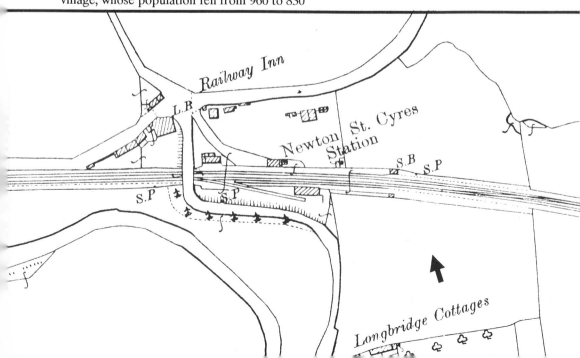

21.　The 08.10 Paddington to Barnstaple speeds through the down platform on 26th June 1971 headed by no.807. On the right is the site of the single goods siding which was closed on 12th September 1960. On 17th August 1930 a 12-lever frame was installed in the booking office in the far end of the building on the left. It was taken out of use on 31st July 1968. Access to the down platform was by a path near the railings on the right. (D.Mitchell)

22.　When photographed in May 1992, only the former LSWR station master's house remained, by then in private ownership. At least the station was still open, with five trains to Exeter calling by request on weekdays. (Mrs.P.Dornom)

CREDITON

23. A standard gauge down train stands near the water column and is about to move to the other side of the broad gauge track. The siding on the left ran to a wagon turntable from which four lines radiated. These and the cattle pen were removed when the platform was lengthened, probably in 1875. (H.C.Casserley coll.)

The 1905 map marks the position of the 5-ton crane (Cr) in the goods yard but does not designate East Box, which is near the timber yard.

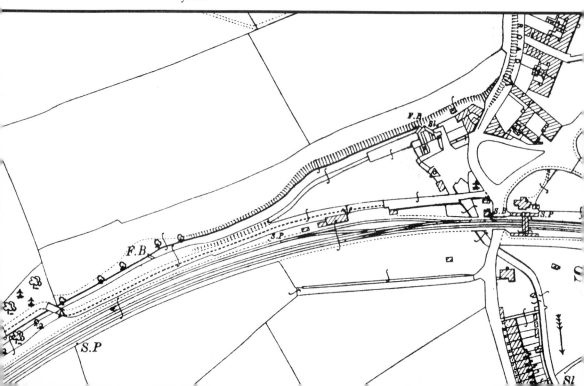

24. This hillside view includes the station approach, the goods shed, nearby industrial buildings, a complete verandah around the station and total roofing of the footbridge. The line has climbed to 135ft above sea level at this location. (Lens of Sutton)

Crediton	1928	1936
No. of passenger tickets issued	19788	8724
No. of season tickets issued	101	112
No. of tickets collected	22448	12898
No. of telegrams	5224	3805
Parcels forwarded	5366	3877
Parcels received	10610	16416
Horses forwarded	37	12
Milk forwarded - cans 1928/gallons 1936	1116	8303
Milk received- cans 1928/gallons 1936	-	21
General goods forwarded (tons)	2674	2173
General goods received (tons)	6339	10465
Coal, Coke etc.	6667	6893
Other minerals forwarded	298	330
Other minerals received	8763	4195
Trucks livestock forwarded	409	364
Trucks livestock received	207	40
Lavatory pennies	264	398

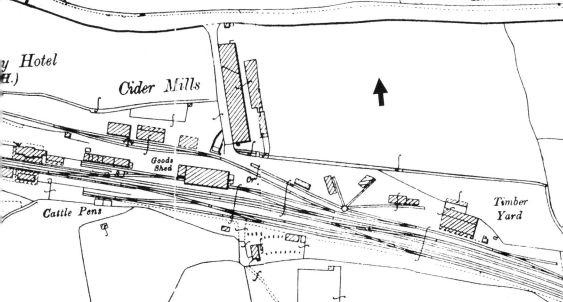

Quarry Cottages

Exeter 7 M.S

y Hotel
d.)

Cider Mills

Goods Shed

Cattle Pens

Timber Yard

25.   When compared with picture 23 it is evident that the platforms were widened after the cessation of broad gauge trains in 1892. Note the road traffic in the down side approach which also served the down yard and cattle pens. (Lens of Sutton)

26. N class no.31837 is piloting no.34032 *Camelford* on the 1.45pm Ilfracombe to Waterloo on 28th August 1954, a peak time for holiday traffic in the last decade before mass motoring. The down sidings seem to have been little used. (S.C.Nash)

27.   Access to the goods shed was from the down line, as down goods trains would be bringing most of the "goods inward". From 1875 this shed was used for transhipment of goods between wagons of different gauges. It contained a crane of 2-ton capacity. This is a 1955 view from the footbridge. (D.Cullum)

28. The 11.00am Waterloo to Ilfracombe ACE was hauled by no.34106 *Lydford* on 30th July 1960, arrival time at the resort being 4.38pm, theoretically. The train had a restaurant car for the entire journey (most shed it at Exeter Central) and included through coaches to Torrington. (S.C.Nash)

29. The north elevation is seen in 1965. At this time the population of the nearby town was about 5000, slightly less than it had been 100 years earlier. Agricultural produce, processed food and cider accounted for much of the traffic here. (J.P.Alsop)

30. No.33033 arrives with the 15.26 from Exeter St.Davids on 1st September 1984 and passes the Western Region type tubular signal posts. This GWR design replaced the LSWR's lattice type seen earlier. Goods facilities were withdrawn on 4th December 1967 and the up yard was later fenced off. These two down sidings were still in place in 1992 and used by the engineers. (D.Mitchell)

31. Barriers came into use on 27th January 1974, being controlled from the adjacent box, which was the only one remaining in use on the route by the time this photograph was taken on 26th November 1990. Railfreight's no.47099 was substituting for a failed DMU on the 14.14 from Barnstaple. The breaker's yard was once occupied by Copp & Co who used an adjacent siding. (D.Mitchell)

32. The 22 levers were superseded by this panel on 16th December 1984. When opened in 1875 this was known as West Box. The 16-lever East Box was near the goods shed and was reduced to a ground frame in 1916. (D.Wilson)

33. The footbridge dates from 1878 and originally had not only full roofing but a barrier along its entire length. This segregated ticket holders crossing between platforms from pedestrians unwilling to wait for the gates to open. (D.Wilson)

34. The 16.15 from Exmouth terminates at Crediton on 19th May 1992. The signalling seen in this and the previous view should be read in conjunction with the panel diagram. The two crossovers in picture no.31 were installed on 17th October 1971 and made Crediton a junction instead of Coleford. From here west there are two parallel single lines - one for Barnstaple trains and the other for stone trains from Meldon Quarry, beyond Okehampton. (Mrs.P.Dornom)

35.   A view towards Exeter includes the ground frame (between the two men on the left), the water column (at the end of the platform) and the 3-road marshalling yard, apparently full. Broad gauge track had been in use here until 1877. (Lens of Sutton)

The 1905 survey marks the ground frame S.B. (above the Cattle Pens). In 1933 it was moved to the east of the loop. The River Yeo runs across the upper part of the map. The "Auction Mart" near the Railway Hotel generated a considerable traffic in livestock on the railway.

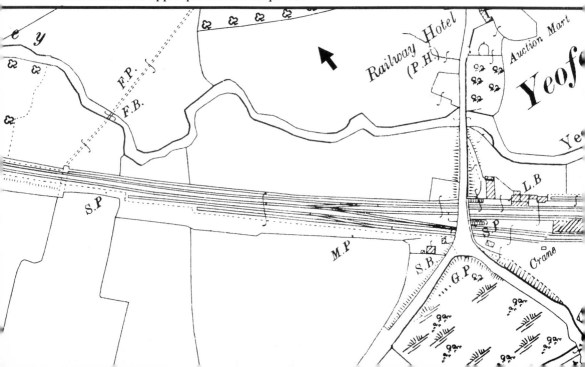

36. Steam rises from the marshalling yard, from the train arrived from Exeter and from a local train loading mail bags in the down bay. Also evident is the 5-ton crane in the goods yard loading timber. Mail carriage ceased in January 1985. (Lens of Sutton)

Yeoford	1928	1936
No. of passenger tickets issued	12807	7842
No. of season tickets issued	30	20
No. of tickets collected	13262	8640
No. of telegrams	4580	2754
Parcels forwarded	538	360
Parcels received	894	640
Horses forwarded	15	4
Milk forwarded - cans 1928/gallons 1936	2080	15458
Milk received - cans 1928/gallons 1936	-	-
General goods forwarded (tons)	895	477
General goods received (tons)	1127	712
Coal, Coke etc.	262	258
Other minerals forwarded	-	23
Other minerals received	1949	447
Trucks livestock forwarded	118	62
Trucks livestock received	70	11
Lavatory pennies	240	207

37. The traffic figures do not reflect the importance of this station as a junction for traffic between North and South Devon. Apart from passengers, there were parcels from Plymouth which would include the "Western Mail" each morning, mailbags and a vast variety of general merchandise. Men and barrows were always on hand for this transfer work. The station house (left) was privately occupied in 1992. (Lens of Sutton)

SOUTHERN RAILWAY.
Issued subject to the Bye-laws, Regulations & Conditions in the Company's Bills and Notices.

Copplestone to
Copplestone   Copplestone
Yeoford   Yeoford

YEOFORD

THIRD CLASS   THIRD CLASS
Fare 8d   Fare 8d
NOT TRANSFERABLE

38. Seen on 14th May 1933, an up express is composed of class T9 no.283 and some then new Maunsell coaches. There is apparently a gap in the parapet wall of the road bridge to give access to the footbridge, as at Mitcham Junction. There was also direct pedestrian access to the up platform, where the booking office was situated. (D.Cullum coll.)

39. Standing in the down bay on 18th August 1954 is another T9, no.30727. Its eight-wheeled tender is coupled to a six-wheeled milk tanker. The eventual provision of crossovers east of the station (probably in WWII) made the bay effectively a loop, but it was not signalled for passenger trains from that direction. (H.C.Casserley)

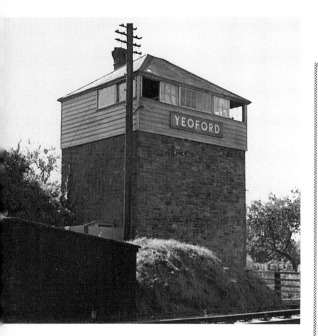

40. The 35-lever box was in use from 1876 until 18th August 1968, the tall base enabling the signalman to see over the adjacent road bridge. Nearly one mile east, Neopardy Box was in use until 7th April 1916. Earlier there was a down trailing siding nearby. (D.Cullum coll.)

Departures Mondays to Fridays June 1960

am

5.54	Ilfracombe
8.8	Salisbury
8.9	Plymouth
8.30	Exeter
9.2	Ilfracombe
9.12	Plymouth
9.23	Exeter
9.58	Waterloo
10.11	Ilfracombe
10.36	Exeter
11.31	Exeter
11.50	Waterloo ACE
11.57	Ilfracombe

pm

12.2	Waterloo ACE
12.20	Plymouth
1.43	Waterloo
1.58	Plymouth
4.15	Okehampton
4.35	Exeter
4.51	Ilfracombe
4.51	Waterloo
5.11	Plymouth
5.25	Waterloo
6.25	Okehampton
6.38	Exeter
6.47	Waterloo
7.5	Plymouth
7.20	Ilfracombe
8.38	Plymouth
9.21	Exeter
9.31	Exeter
10.50	Plymouth

The 11.57 and 12.2 ACE departures were joined at Exeter Central. Most Ilfracombe trains carried Torrington portions. Also noteworthy is the long break in the afternoon.

41. A down Ilfracombe train on 16th August 1958 is piloted by no.34069 *Hawkinge*, the train engine being N class no.31833. In 1942-43, the marshalling yard was doubled to six parallel sidings to meet wartime traffic requirements. The facing crossover from the down line is barely visible. It was taken out of use in 1952 but not removed until 1962. (A.E.Bennett)

42. The signal box is behind the photographer as Ivatt class 2 no.41318 arrives with the 3.55pm Lapford to Crediton freight service on 7th May 1960. The post was used at night to carry a pressurised oil light of the Tilley type. (S.C.Nash)

43. The platform lampposts were fitted with equipment for hoisting and stabilising Tilley lamps which were vastly superior to the simple wick type. Beyond the down side buildings in this 1964 photograph is a steel bridge over two tracks. This replaced a brick arch similar to the remaining two. The roof of the signal box is visible beyond it. (C.L.Caddy)

44. A view from the bridge in July 1972 includes no.7504 with an Exeter to Barnstaple service. By then the other track was used exclusively by stone trains and the canopy no longer carried the sign *REFRESHMENTS* seen in pictures 36 and 37. The goods yard closed on 10th February 1962 and the sidings were taken out of use in 1968. (D.Mitchell)

45.   This picture was taken exactly ten years after the previous one and reveals that the remaining passenger platform has one electric light. The railings surround an area once boarded. The River Troney passes under the tracks here, evidence of bridges being included in pictures 35, 38, 43 and 44. The locomotive is no.31131. (D.Mitchell)

46.   A narrow bodied class 33 with stone from Meldon Quarry approaches Yeoford in August 1989. The line to Okehampton and the quarry runs in a valley beyond the hilltop village of Colebrooke, seen in the background. (J.A.M.Vaughan)

COLEFORD JUNCTION

47. Viewed from a down train in 1969, the box was in use from 1st October 1873 until 17th October 1971 and was fitted with a 13-lever frame. The houses are in the village of Penstone. A crossover was situated on the Yeoford side of the junction, this being mainly for the benefit of the engineers. (D.J.Aston)

48. No.31152 takes the former up line to Barnstaple on 3rd July 1982, while in the foreground we see the former down line to Okehampton. This 20 chain curve was subject to a 20mph speed restriction in its last years as part of a junction. (D.Mitchell)

COPPLESTONE

49.   A postcard view towards Barnstaple includes the 1887 water tank, the goods shed (with curved doorway) and the slaughterhouse in the distance. The census returns for Copplestone and Yeoford were combined with Colebrooke, both being in that parish. The figures were 787 for 1871 and 415 for 1971, explaining the poor passenger figures. (Lens of Sutton)

50.   Waiting for the up starter to clear on 27th June 1949 is an unlettered 0-6-0 of class 0395. This engine was built in 1885 as LSWR no.29, ran as SR no.3029 from 1935 and as BR no. 30564 from 1951 until scrapped in 1958. The leading vehicle reminds us that milk was an important traffic in the area. (J.H.Aston)

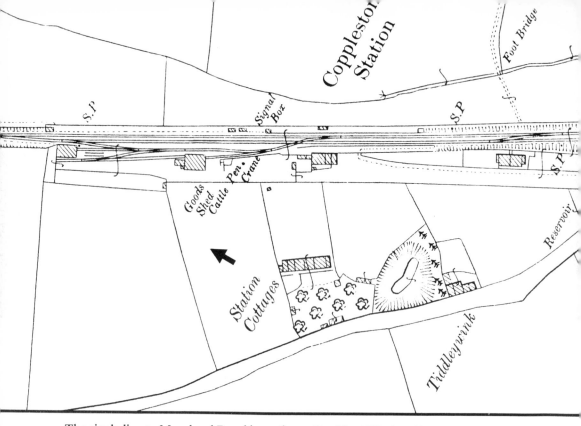

The single line to Morchard Road is on the left of this 1905 map. Here is the summit of the route, 350ft above sea level. As at most other stations on the route, there was generous provision of cranage - 5 tons in the yard and 2 tons in the shed.

51. The 1873 signal box had ten levers and was in use until 1971 when the line was singled southwards. Its doubling had been undertaken in 1883 but this was never continued northwards. A water crane stands at the end of the down platform, supplied from the tank seen in the previous picture. This was the scene in January 1965. (C.L.Caddy)

Copplestone	1928	1936
No. of passenger tickets issued	4224	2377
No. of season tickets issued	8	10
No. of tickets collected	5226	3310
No. of telegrams	1642	578
Parcels forwarded	371	504
Parcels received	1171	1083
Horses forwarded	-	1
Milk forwarded - cans 1928/gallons 1936	20	308
Milk received - cans 1928/gallons 1936	-	-
General goods forwarded (tons)	1784	558
General goods received (tons)	2449	5076
Coal, Coke etc.	465	321
Other minerals forwarded	-	804
Other minerals received	1634	860
Trucks livestock forwarded	191	160
Trucks livestock received	73	12
Lavatory pennies	-	-

52. No.33014 passes through with the 15.00 Exeter St.Davids to Barnstaple on 11th February 1985. The up line had been retained as far as the bridge in the background, where it was slewed in 1971 to connect with the down track. (C.Hall)

53. This is typical of the substantial stone buildings provided from the outset by the NDR. On the left of this 1992 picture is the former entrance to the goods yard, which closed to traffic on 6th September 1965. (Mrs. P.Dornom)

54. A northward view from Morchard Road bridge includes the down siding which has a dock once used in connection with a nearby slaughterhouse. The passing of long trains in the holiday season sometimes necessitated reversal into this siding. (D.Cullum)

55. This, the previous and the next photograph were all taken on 3rd August 1955. The architectural similarity of the NDR stations is noteworthy and has justified their retention, albeit in private hands. It is about two miles to Morchard Bishop. (D.Cullum)

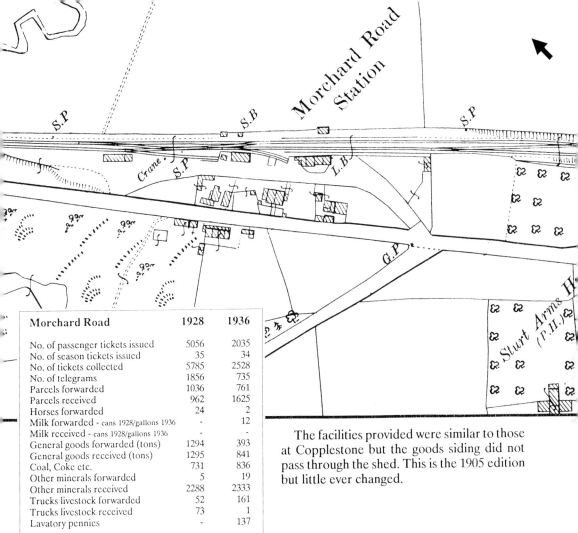

Morchard Road	1928	1936
No. of passenger tickets issued	5056	2035
No. of season tickets issued	35	34
No. of tickets collected	5785	2528
No. of telegrams	1856	735
Parcels forwarded	1036	761
Parcels received	962	1625
Horses forwarded	24	2
Milk forwarded - cans 1928/gallons 1936	-	12
Milk received - cans 1928/gallons 1936	-	-
General goods forwarded (tons)	1294	393
General goods received (tons)	1295	841
Coal, Coke etc.	731	836
Other minerals forwarded	5	19
Other minerals received	2288	2333
Trucks livestock forwarded	52	161
Trucks livestock received	73	1
Lavatory pennies	-	137

The facilities provided were similar to those at Copplestone but the goods siding did not pass through the shed. This is the 1905 edition but little ever changed.

(663)

SOUTH WESTERN RAILWAY.
FOR DROVERS OR DEALERS.
THIRD CLASS.

No. 99   Station _____ 187___

PASS CREDITON _____ , by _____ o'clock Train,

from _____ to _____ , in charge

of _____ the property

of Mr. _____ , of _____

AVAILABLE FOR ONE JOURNEY ONLY.

This Ticket is required to be shown to the attendant by the passenger on taking his seat, and must be delivered to the Ticket Collector at the end of the journey.

This Ticket is issued to, and accepted by the Holder, subject to the conditions on the back.

56.   Here is an example of the unprofitable freight operations that occurred in the mid-1950s. Goods facilities at this station were withdrawn on 30th December 1963. The loop and signal box closed on 6th March 1964. (D.Cullum)

57.   The up line appears little used in this 1962 picture. In earlier years there were regularly three trains here simultaneously. At 9.11am the 7.45 from Torrington was due; at 9.09 the 8.23 from Exeter (Queen Street) was scheduled and the up freight from Barnstaple had to be held in the yard. Note the broad gauge separation of platforms. (Pamlin Prints)

58.   By February 1966 only the goods shed remained to suggest that this was once an important place in the commercial life of the district. The connection from the down line to the goods shed had been removed back in 1931. (C.L.Caddy)

59.   By the time this photograph was taken on 19th May 1992, Sprinters were monopolising the service, providing a fast and comfortable means of reaching the centre of the City of Exeter. The ballast marks the site of the short dock siding. (Mrs.P.Dornom)

LAPFORD

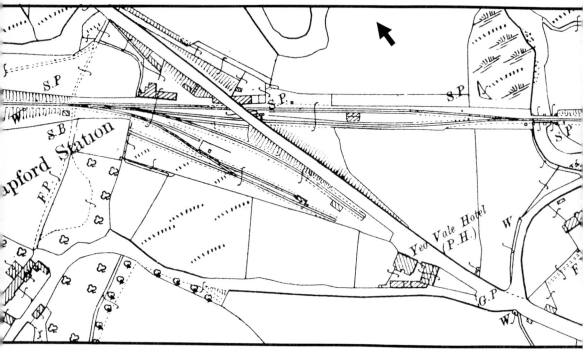

The main building and the up platform is to the left of the road bridge on this 1905 map, while the down platform occupies an island position to the right of it. Note that there was then no road access to the up side.

60. This classical Edwardian postcard view of the up side is worthy of repetition. The nearby village is of great charm and has changed little. The population was 683 in 1871 and 681 in 1971. The engine is an Adams class 460 4-4-0. (D.Cullum coll.)

61. Viewed from a short up train standing at the platform, class N 2-6-0 no.1409 starts away for Barnstaple on 25th May 1935. The cart crossing gave access to the up platform from the goods yard. Unusually there was no crane in this yard. (H.C.Casserley)

62. The 9.42am from Exeter Central is held by the signal at the down platform awaiting the arrival of the 9.0am from Ilfracombe, headed by class N no.1406. The wooden building and the adjacent bridge arch were used as a slaughterhouse for many years. (J.R.W.Kirkby)

Lapford	1928	1936
No. of passenger tickets issued	6400	4566
No. of season tickets issued	37	36
No. of tickets collected	7448	5389
No. of telegrams	1488	1373
Parcels forwarded	1495	1120
Parcels received	2009	2087
Horses forwarded	17	4
Milk forwarded - cans 1928/gallons 1936	4181	-
Milk received - cans 1928/gallons 1936	9700	24624
General goods forwarded (tons)	1483	1947
General goods received (tons)	2135	3059
Coal, Coke etc.	1083	3164
Other minerals forwarded	70	19
Other minerals received	1575	2000
Trucks livestock forwarded	186	165
Trucks livestock received	86	7
Lavatory pennies	-	139

SOUTHERN RAILWAY.

ONE BICYCLE AT OWNER'S RISK
(accompanied by Passenger)

Lapford to (D.O)

6D ANY STATION
NOT EXCEEDING
10 MILES.

This ticket is available for one journey only
and must be given up at destination Station

FOR CONDITIONS SEE BACK

0028

63. The signalman has left his 13-lever box to present the Tyer's tablet to the driver of the southbound express. The scenic beauty is enhanced by the station name set into the bank. Public goods services ceased on 4th December 1967. (A.F.E.Field)

64. All structures were extended for double track in the 1900s but never received it. See also the bridges in the previous two pictures. These points were worked by a porter from a 2-lever ground frame situated by the pole behind the down waiting shelter. (D.Cullum)

65. The loop and down platform were added in 1873 but space constraints resulted in the latter being sited in this inconvenient position. The building included a small ticket office which was manned briefly before the departure of down trains. (A.F.E.Field)

66. The signal box closed on 21st June 1970 and two ground frames were installed, one adjacent to the points at either end of the loop. This was subsequently only used by freight or engineers trains. No.50042 is seen working a DMU substitution service on 19th July 1990. By then the building had been sold and a bus shelter provided for passengers. (D.Mitchell)

67. No.47280 backs onto empty fertiliser wagons on 16th September 1991, prior to running round them in the loop and returning to Exeter Riverside. The buildings in the background were in use for the manufacture of Ambrosia milk products from 1928 until 1970. This was a big source of railway revenue, both from milk in and finished products out. The siding was used for grain and timber, in addition to fertiliser, and was still open for traffic when required in 1993. (D.Mitchell)

68. DMU no.823 is passing the site of the down platform as it proceeds towards Exeter. The south ground frame is in the distance, close to the bridge over the River Yeo. (D.Wilson)

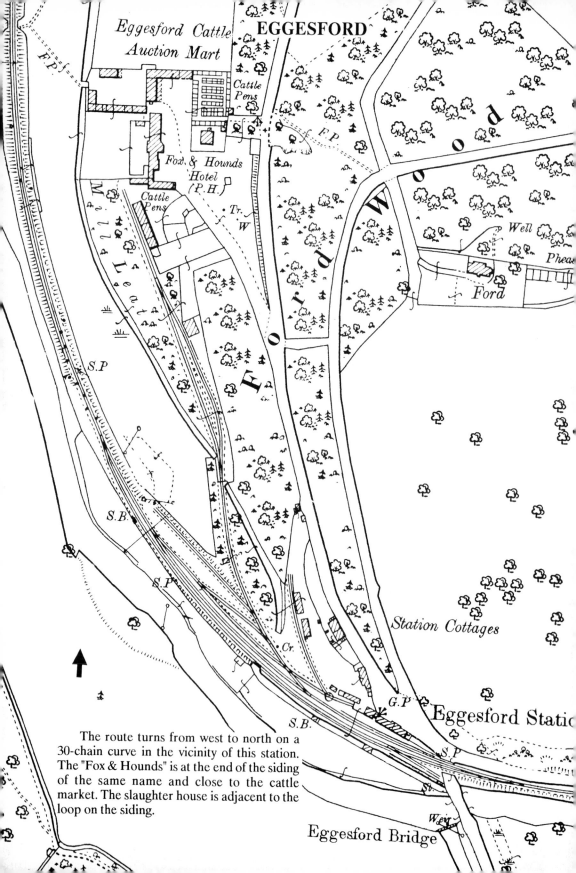

EGGESFORD

Eggesford Cattle
Auction Mart

Cattle
Pens

Fox & Hounds
Hotel
(P.H.)

Cattle
Pens

F o r d   W o o d

Well

Phea

Ford

Tr
W

F.P.

Mill Leat

S.P.

S.B.

S.P.

Cr.

Station Cottages

G.P.

S.B.

Eggesford Statio

S.P.

St.

Wer

The route turns from west to north on a
30-chain curve in the vicinity of this station.
The "Fox & Hounds" is at the end of the siding
of the same name and close to the cattle
market. The slaughter house is adjacent to the
loop on the siding.

Eggesford Bridge

69. While the up platform has the impressive multi-gabled stone building, the down side has a waiting shelter and signal box, both timber framed. This 1955 panorama is from the level crossing. (D.Cullum)

70. A 1960 picture records the co-acting up starting signals, the upper one being provided so that drivers of non-stop trains could see it above the buildings before reaching the station. The level crossing gates were locked from the signal box but worked by hand. (H.C.Casserley coll.)

71. Hens flee as no.34109 *Sir Trafford Leigh-Mallory* arrives from Barnstaple on 16th August 1958. The flat wagon beside the 7½-ton crane is awaiting a container, the siding continuing to the right to the "Fox & Hounds". The Anglo American Oil Co. had a depot here and other tankers also arrived with bitumen for the nearby quarry. The yard closed on 4th January 1965. (A.E.Bennett)

Eggesford	1928	1936
No. of passenger tickets issued	9040	4304
No. of season tickets issued	36	42
No. of tickets collected	10176	5480
No. of telegrams	2408	- ●
Parcels forwarded	1702	739
Parcels received	4461	5076
Horses forwarded	62	23
Milk forwarded - cans 1928/gallons 1936	-	-
Milk received - cans 1928/gallons 1936	-	-
General goods forwarded (tons)	2792	1053
General goods received (tons)	2491	2537
Coal, Coke etc.	1195	925
Other minerals forwarded	9	38
Other minerals received	2244	1686
Trucks livestock forwarded	292	135
Trucks livestock received	24	10
Lavatory pennies	348	432
● - Telegraph instruments abolished		

72. A 1962 record shows that the up starting signals had been replaced by one on a short rail-built post. Sighting problems were solved by the provision of a banner repeater signal on the post on the left. The dock siding (left) was only 40yds long but the "Fox & Hounds" was 363yds in length. (H.C.Casserley)

73. Booking office windows were small on security grounds but this had the unintentional effect of creating a fierce draught in winter, when the office fire was alight, resulting in passengers' paper money becoming airborne, inwards. Guards have collected fares at intermediate stations since 30th September 1968. (C.Hall)

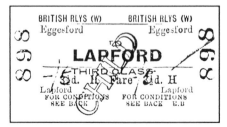

BRITISH RLYS (W)   BRITISH RLYS (W)
Eggesford   Eggesford
LAPFORD
THIRD CLASS
3d. H. Fare 3d. H
Lapford   Lapford
FOR CONDITIONS   FOR CONDITIONS
SEE BACK   SEE BACK E.B
868   868

SOUTHERN RAILWAY.
This Ticket is issued subject to the By-laws
Regulations & Conditions stated in the
Company's Time Tables Bills & Notices
Available on DAY of issue ONLY
LAPFORD to
Lapford   Lapford
Eggesford   Eggesford
EGGESFORD
Third Class   Third Class
Fare 5½d   Fare 5½d
9380   9380

74. The earlier signal box and the loop were closed on 21st November 1967 following flood damage. This replacement came into use on 28th September 1969, along with a new down platform. Controlled lifting barriers were in operation from 30th November of that year. Token exchange is taking place on 3rd July 1982. The box was formerly in use at Ashington Junction, near High Wycombe. (D.Mitchell)

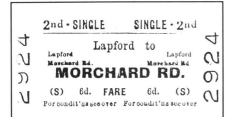

2nd · SINGLE   SINGLE · 2nd

Lapford to

Lapford   Lapford
Morchard Rd.   Morchard Rd
MORCHARD RD.

(S)   6d.   FARE   6d.   (S)
For condit'ns see over   For condit'ns see over

2924

SOUTHERN RAILWAY.
Issued subject to the Bye-laws, Regulations &
Conditions in the Company's Bills and Notices.

Copplestone to

Morchard Rd

Via

First Class. Fare
NOT TRANSFERABLE   4ᵈ

0068   0900

75.   The cottage style of building harmonises well with its rural surroundings, the population of the village having more than halved to 69 in the 100 years to 1971. The relatively high figures for tickets issued shows that the station serves a large district. (Mrs.P.Dornom)

76.   The signal box closed on 1st December 1987, since when drivers have obtained tokens from the cupboards at the end of each platform and conductors have operated the barrier controls, as seen here on 23rd May 1992. Until 1936 there was a short siding in the left foreground. (D.Wilson)

KINGS NYMPTON

77. Unusually for a postcard, staff are seen in "action". Platelayers are leaning on their shovels and a carpenter rests against the fence while new poster boards lean against the building. Passenger figures here were limited by the drop in village inhabitants from 642 in 1871 to 336 in 1971. (Lens of Sutton)

South Molton Road	1928	1936
(Kings Nympton on map)		
No. of passenger tickets issued	6245	3645
No. of season tickets issued	11	38
No. of tickets collected	6779	4209
No. of telegrams	1517	570
Parcels forwarded	1649	949
Parcels received	2057	2432
Horses forwarded	34	6
Milk forwarded - cans 1928/gallons 1936	-	12641
Milk received - cans 1928/gallons 1936	-	-
General goods forwarded (tons)	2072	655
General goods received (tons)	2273	3016
Coal, Coke etc.	806	1136
Other minerals forwarded	6	14
Other minerals received	2972	2413
Trucks livestock forwarded	361	143
Trucks livestock received	38	-
Lavatory pennies	-	276

The 1905 map shows a layout that remained unchanged for the subsequent 60 years. A cattle market was held monthly near the "Fortescue Arms", this event generating some additional rail revenue.

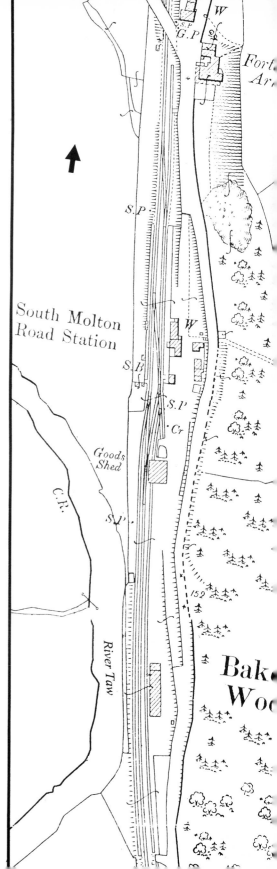

78. Class N 2-6-0 no.1408 is working the 1.0pm from Waterloo on a wet day in August 1938. It was that West Country rain that nourished the lush pastures, that fed the cows, that produced the milk that filled the churns that are seen on the right and in so many traffic returns for the area. (D.H.Wakely/J.R.W.Kirkby coll.)

79. The long evening shadows on 22nd August 1951 make the bogie coaches look like early four-wheelers. An inquisitive youngster is approaching the new nameboard, fitted on 1st March 1951 when the name "South Molton Road" was changed. It was dropped on the ground and surmounted by a board bearing the word "Formerly". (N.W.Sprinks)

80. The 16-lever signal box dated from 1st October 1873 and remained in use until 26th July 1970. Beyond it is the water tank adjacent to the River Taw, which joins the Little Dart River about two miles south of the station. The River Mole flows through South Molton, which is about eight miles north-eastwards, and joins the Taw north of the station. The route has often been subjected to flooding. (A.F.E.Field)

81. No.34030 *Watersmeet* (apt for this locality) runs in with the 2.15pm from Torrington on 3rd August 1955. It combined with the 2.20 from Ilfracombe at Barnstaple Junction. The train called at all stations to Lapford, then Crediton, Exeter St.Davids and Central where it was coupled to the waiting Plymouth portion. It left at 4.30pm and was due at Waterloo at 8.25. (D.Cullum)

82. A southward view from the A377 bridge in 1955 emphasises the great space between the tracks, normally known as the "six-foot". This was a legacy from the broad gauge era, which ended here in 1877. The local coal merchant was appropriately J.Cole & Sons. (D.Cullum)

83. Another 1955 picture shows the connection which enabled down goods trains to shunt the yard. While the up starter is clearly upper quadrant on lattice post, the down is lower quadrant on wooden post, both features being of an earlier era. (D.Cullum)

84. The goods yard ceased to handle general traffic on 4th December 1967 and the shed was soon demolished. There had been 2 and 5 ton cranes, as at most stations on the route. A shed siding was retained until 1981 for fertiliser traffic. (A.E.Bennett)

85. The loop was taken out of use when the signal box closed in 1970. Apart from the addition of a dormer window above the former booking office, little has changed. (D.Wilson)

PORTSMOUTH ARMS

86. The single siding goods yard was provided with a 5-ton crane but no goods shed, this being located on the up platform, just beyond the waiting room on the left. The station master's house is largely obscured by the down buildings. (D.Cullum)

```
┌─────────────────────────────────────────┐
│  BRITISH RLYS (W)    BRITISH RLYS (W)     │
│  PortsmouthArms  PortsmouthArms           │
│            TO                             │
│       KINGS NYMPTON                       │
│  ─────────────────────────────────────   │
│       THIRD CLASS                         │
│       8d.Z Fare 8d.  Z                    │
│  Kings Nympton      Kings Nympton         │
│  FOR CONDITIONS   FOR CONDITIONS          │
│    SEE BACK         SEE BACK  T.U         │
└─────────────────────────────────────────┘
```
(ticket numbered 004 on both ends)

Portsmouth Arms	1928	1936
No. of passenger tickets issued	4997	3357
No. of season tickets issued	-	6
No. of tickets collected	5873	4042
No. of telegrams	506	225
Parcels forwarded	853	814
Parcels received	1115	1243
Horses forwarded	11	15
Milk forwarded - cans 1928/gallons 1936	-	3434
Milk received - cans 1928/gallons 1936	-	-
General goods forwarded (tons)	859	243
General goods received (tons)	1132	1879
Coal, Coke etc.	425	962
Other minerals forwarded	-	103 ●
Other minerals received	1179	541
Trucks livestock forwarded	245	175
Trucks livestock received	45	5
Lavatory pennies	-	200

● - Pig manure to Braunton

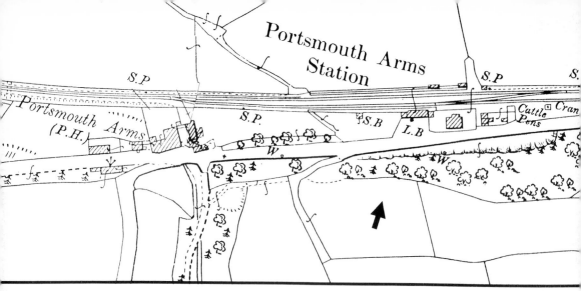

The 1905 edition has the only siding on the right, below the main line. It was 272yds long and could accommodate 40 wagons.

87. No.34015 *Exmouth* passes the nameboard on 16th August 1958. The name was taken from the nearby public house, itself named after the Earl of Portsmouth who was involved in financing the adjacent turnpike road in a previous transport era. (A.E.Bennett)

88. As elsewhere on the route, the "six-foot" was much greater than that, but, unlike at several of the other passing places, the loop was of a reasonable length. It was 138yds long and could take eight coaches, only peak holiday trains exceeding this. This and the next two photographs were taken on 27th August 1962. (Pamlin Prints)

89. A water can stands outside the 10-lever box, which had no associated ground frames. The 1873 box and up loop were taken out of use on 3rd April 1966. The goods siding closed on 3rd July 1961 and was lifted at the end of 1963. (Pamlin Prints)

90.   Three smart Bulleid-designed coaches depart towards Barnstaple, showing their steam heating and vacuum brake hoses, now features almost entirely relegated to preserved railways. The buck-eye coupling is in the down position. (Pamlin Prints)

91.   The 3.0pm from Ilfracombe passes over the 64yd long Kingford Viaduct as it approaches Portsmouth Arms on 3rd August 1955. The Taw Valley, and in consequence the railway, has a series of reverse curves in this vicinity, at 25 to 30 chains radius. This train combined with a Plymouth portion at Exeter Central, departing at 5.53 for Waterloo. (D.Cullum)

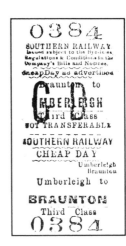

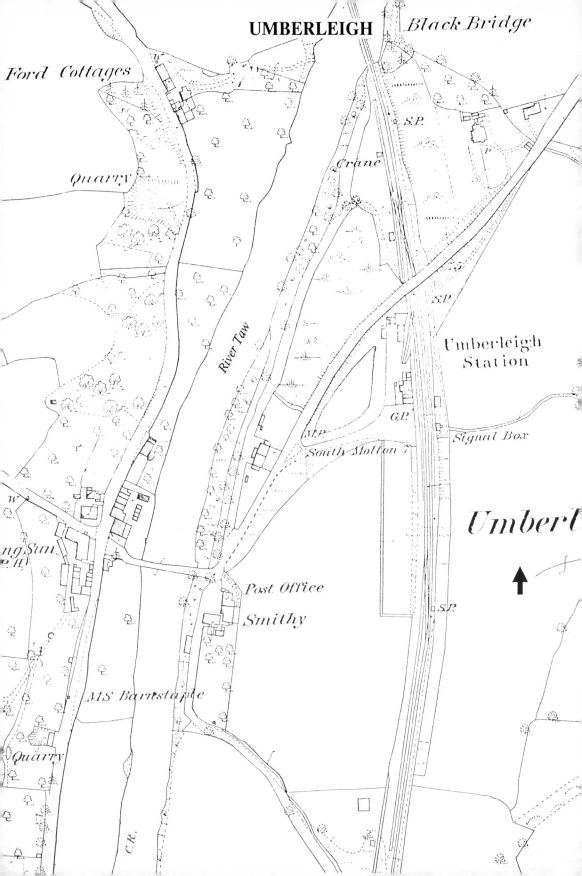

92. This northward view includes the signal box which opened on 19th October 1890 when the double track northward to Pill Bridge came into use. It replaced an 1873 model of the type seen elsewhere. (Lens of Sutton)

The 1888 map indicates the arrangement prior to track doubling northwards.

93. Camping coaches were common in South Devon but rare further north. Ex-LCDR no. 1619, seen on 30th June 1948, was later replaced by an ex-LSWR bogie coach. (J.H.Aston)

Umberleigh	1928	1936
No. of passenger tickets issued	9327	8820
No. of season tickets issued	10	115 ●
No. of tickets collected	10544	10026
No. of telegrams	1296	427
Parcels forwarded	1026	725
Parcels received	1339	1889
Horses forwarded	20	2
Milk forwarded - cans 1928/gallons 1936	-	-
Milk received - cans 1928/gallons 1936	-	-
General goods forwarded (tons)	520	218
General goods received (tons)	939	816
Coal, Coke etc.	989	823
Other minerals forwarded	268	12
Other minerals received	500	454
Trucks livestock forwarded	162	112
Trucks livestock received	13	-
Lavatory pennies	-	350
● - Camping coach		

94. Rolling hills surround the entire route giving arriving holidaymakers a foretaste of the heavenly coastline to come. An August 1956 panorama includes the end and side loading dock used occasionally for agricultural machinery. The goods shed door is above the catch point, an awkward arrangement. (Wessex coll.)

95. The signal box had 31 levers and was in communication with the box south at Umberleigh Gates. This was a ground frame and closed on 19th November 1972. The line north was singled and the box closed on 21st May 1971. (D.Cullum)

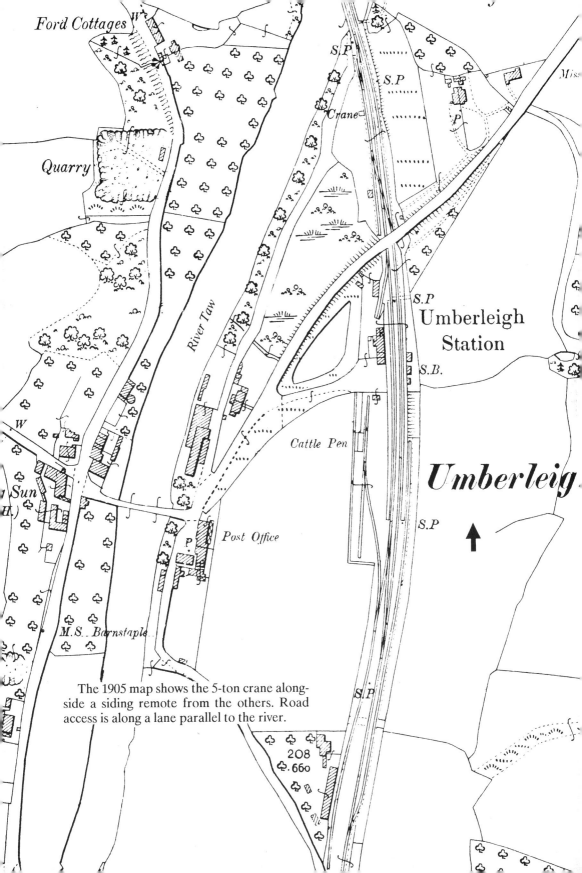

Ford Cottages

Quarry

River Taw

W

Sun
H.)

Post Office

M.S. Barnstaple

S.P

S.P

S.P

Crane

P

S.P Umberleigh
Station

S.B.

Umberleig

Cattle Pen

S.P

S.P

208
.660

The 1905 map shows the 5-ton crane alongside a siding remote from the others. Road
access is along a lane parallel to the river.

96.   Looking north from the road bridge in 1956, we note that the location was used by the permanent way department. This still applied in 1992 when one gang was in charge of the northern part of the route. The goods yard closed on 4th January 1965. (D.Cullum)

97. Class 4 2-6-4Ts nos.80043 and 80039 stand by the up starter and are about to leave with the Southern Counties Touring Society's special on 3rd October 1965. It had visited Ilfracombe and Torrington to mark the cessation of passenger services to the latter place. A refuge siding had earlier been in use on the right. Torrington is about seven miles by road from here but 21 by rail. (S.C.Nash)

98. The 11.15 Exeter St.Davids to Barnstaple passes through on 23rd March 1982. Little had changed ten years later. Beyond the bridge the track was slewed so that the former up line could be used on the next bridge over the river. (D.Mitchell)

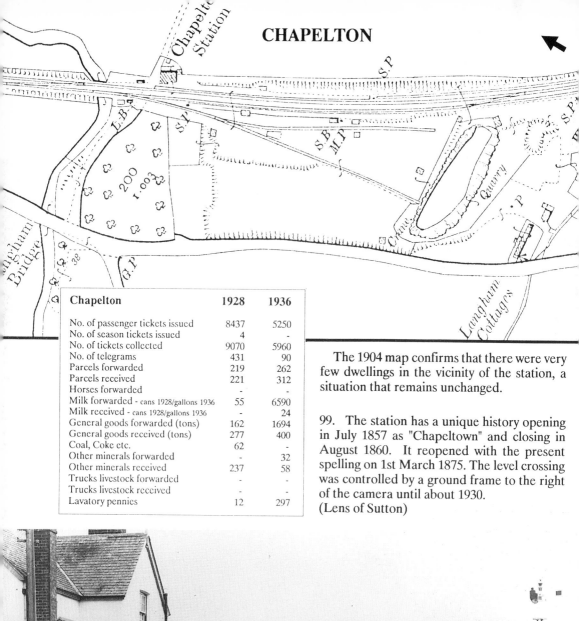

CHAPELTON

Chapelton	1928	1936
No. of passenger tickets issued	8437	5250
No. of season tickets issued	4	-
No. of tickets collected	9070	5960
No. of telegrams	431	90
Parcels forwarded	219	262
Parcels received	221	312
Horses forwarded	-	-
Milk forwarded - cans 1928/gallons 1936	55	6590
Milk received - cans 1928/gallons 1936	-	24
General goods forwarded (tons)	162	1694
General goods received (tons)	277	400
Coal, Coke etc.	62	-
Other minerals forwarded	-	32
Other minerals received	237	58
Trucks livestock forwarded	-	-
Trucks livestock received	-	-
Lavatory pennies	12	297

The 1904 map confirms that there were very few dwellings in the vicinity of the station, a situation that remains unchanged.

99. The station has a unique history opening in July 1857 as "Chapeltown" and closing in August 1860. It reopened with the present spelling on 1st March 1875. The level crossing was controlled by a ground frame to the right of the camera until about 1930.
(Lens of Sutton)

100.   Seen in 1956, the platforms have standard separation as there was no loop here prior to the doubling of the line on 19th October 1890, also the date of the opening of the 23-lever signal box. This closed on 26th January 1966 and the up line was taken out of use on 21st May 1971. The sidings closed on 4th January 1965. (D.Cullum)

101.   Approaching the oil-lit up platform on 29th August 1956 is no.34014 *Budleigh Salterton* with the 2.20pm from Ilfracombe. The two sidings handled little traffic until 1930 when Chappell & Walton established their timber yard adjacent to them. A 10-ton crane was in use loading a variety of products including fencing, pit props and timber for railway wagon construction. (D.Cullum)

102. A single car class 153 works the 16.18 from Barnstaple on 24th July 1992, having recently been converted from a two-car class 155 set. From May 1986 until October 1987, class 142 "Skipper" or "Pacer" units were in use but their four-wheeled rigid wheelbase was found to be unsatisfactory on the winding lines of Devon. (D.Wilson)

103. The owner of the former station house and office has added a canopy and displays an SR-style nameboard. The remaining four mile stretch to Barnstaple is almost straight, an unusual feature of the route which has been promoted as the "Tarka Line" since 1990. The lineside rivers contain a high proportion of England's otters. (D.Wilson)

SOUTHERN RAILWAY

TOUR NORTH DEVON & NORTH CORNWALL

WITH A
7-DAY "HOLIDAY" SEASON

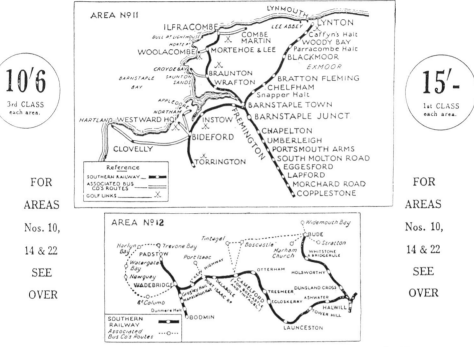

10/6
3rd CLASS
each area.

15/-
1st CLASS
each area.

FOR AREAS Nos. 10, 14 & 22 SEE OVER

FOR AREAS Nos. 10, 14 & 22 SEE OVER

The Cheapest Way to Explore the Beauties of North Devon and North Cornwall

is by using a
local 7-DAY "HOLIDAY" SEASON, issued
DAILY from March 29th until October 31st, 1934, at
ANY S.R. STATION shown on the above maps.

The Tickets are available by ANY TRAIN at ANY S.R.
STATION in the area, for 7 days, including date of issue.

*Fares do not include cost of Road Travel. No allowance or extension of date can be granted
on these tickets in consequence of there being no Sunday Service of Trains in certain areas.*

CHILDREN UNDER 14—HALF PRICE

Travel WHEN --
WHERE --
and AS OFTEN as you like

*Local 7-Day "Holiday" Season Tickets may also be obtained in advance at S.R. London Termini and Agents.
Season Tickets for Dogs and Bicycles accompanying Passengers holding 7-Day "Holiday" Season Tickets are issued at the
following charges:—Dog 2/6 per week, Bicycle 5/- per week.
For details of 7-Day "Holiday" Seasons covering other areas, get handbills at the Local S.R. Stations and Offices.*

Waterloo Station, S.E. 1.
March, 1934.

H. A. WALKER,
General Manager.

C.X. 459/— 88/12Ms

Waterlow & Sons Limited, London, Dunstable & Watford.

BARNSTAPLE JUNCTION

The 1932 edition has been reduced to 20" to 1 mile to include the line to Exeter (lower right), the 1887 spur to the GWR (above it), the line to Fremington and Torrington (lower left) and the railway viaduct and road bridge to Barnstaple Town (top left). There are two sidings from the SR into the industrial area, a former shipyard. They were in use from WWI until 30th November 1967, serving Saw Milling & General Supplies who supplied sawn timber for aircraft components in WWII. The lines also carried cement in and concrete products out.

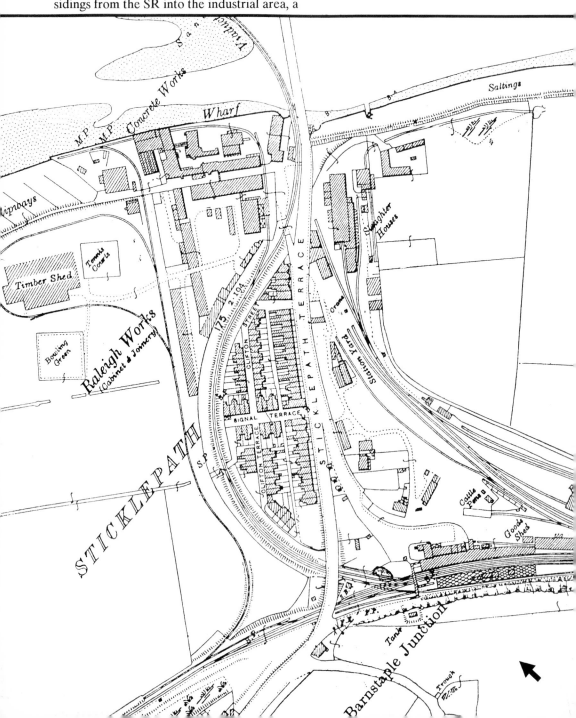

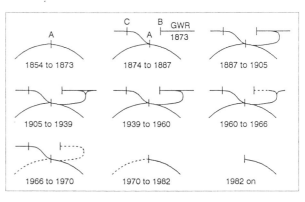

Barnstaple station names
A "Junction" 1874 to 1971
B "Victoria Road" from 1949
C "Town" from 1886
Dashes indicate freight only.
The narrow gauge Lynton & Barnstaple line is not shown but is described in detail in our *Branch Line to Lynton* album.

Barnstaple Junction	1928	1936
No. of passenger tickets issued	64346	32070
No. of season tickets issued	11	217
No. of tickets collected	114417	76865
No. of telegrams	21038	15378
Parcels forwarded	8597	7280
Parcels received	29181	37661
Horses forwarded	94	42
Milk forwarded - cans 1928/gallons 1936	-	595
Milk received - cans 1928/gallons 1936	-	8639
General goods forwarded (tons)	8160	5810
General goods received (tons)	17860	15645
Coal, Coke etc.	16714	23293
Other minerals forwarded	1972	2848
Other minerals received	7703	17841
Trucks livestock forwarded	629	471
Trucks livestock received	513	101
Lavatory pennies	2772	5717

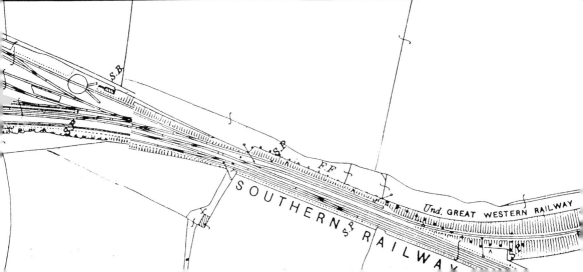

104. A northward view over the River Taw to Barnstaple includes a broad gauge train of the type that started running from Exeter on 1st August 1854. Freight services between Fremington and Barnstaple had commenced in August 1848. Dual gauge track was completed on 2nd March 1863. (R.C.Riley coll.)

105. On the left of this picture (taken from the road bridge) is a salmon and brown LSWR coach which is largely obscuring the curves of the Ilfracombe line. The short sidings on the left and right were lost in later alterations. (Lens of Sutton)

106. A closer examination at the staff crossing also reveals the anatomy of a goods van. The date of the event was not recorded. The symbol "T" by the footbridge indicated the termination of the permanent speed restriction. (Lens of Sutton)

107. In 1924 the hill on the left was cut back to make room for an additional track and the down platform subsequently became an island. Seen on the left is class N no. A861 on 21st July 1925, the year in which this class was introduced to the route. Later they were fitted with smoke deflectors. On the right is class A12 0-4-2 no.E628 shunting the goods yard. It was in use from 1893 until 1938. (H.C.Casserley)

108. This picture continues from the previous one and features the two-road engine shed with its adjacent machine shop, stores and office. Sixteen locomotives were allocated here at the end of the LSWR era. (A.B.McLeod)

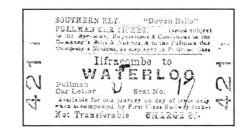

109. Seen in July 1925 is class 0460 no.0475 still bearing its LSWR number. It was withdrawn in the following year. Two boilersmiths and five fitters were on the staff for many years and the workshop had a lathe and milling machine for running repairs. (H.C.Casserley)

110. The up "Atlantic Coast Express" is headed by no.34021 *Dartmoor* on 25th May 1957. The train carried through coaches from Torrington and Ilfracombe, with others joining later in the journey from Padstow, Bude, Plymouth and Yeovil Town. A restaurant car was attached at Exeter Central. (T.Wright)

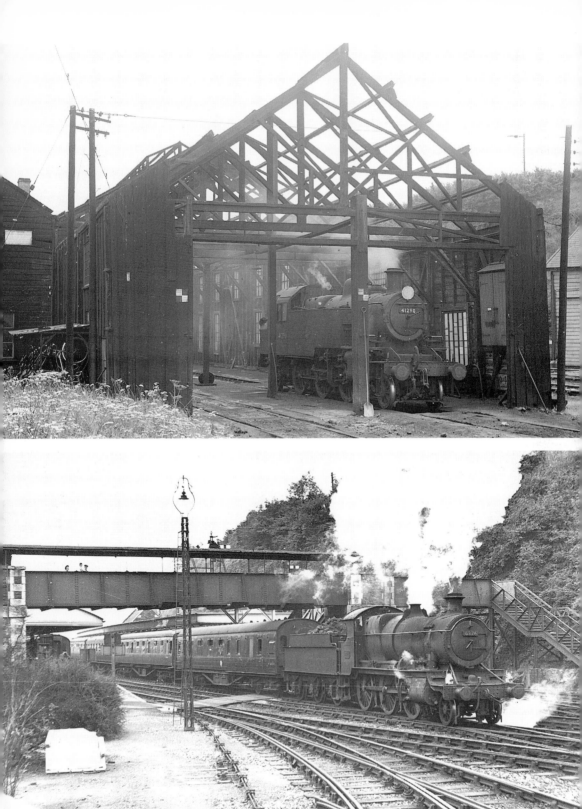

111. Following the closure of the nearby Western Region depot in 1952 and Torrington shed in 1959, over 100 men and 28 locomotives were allocated here. The end of steam was imminent when class 2 2-6-2T no.41290 was photographed on 25th July 1964. By 1968 there were only ten crew, signing-on ceasing here in 1971. (J.H.Aston)

BARNSTAPLE JUNCTION

113. On the same day ex-GWR no.6345 appears with the 10.12 Ilfracombe to Cardiff service. In the background is "B" Box, which was West Box until 2nd October 1949. It replaced the 1874 box in 1924, its 40-lever frame being in use until 21st May 1971. (E.Wilmshurst)

112. Western Region locomotives started running through to Torrington in 1952, although there had been through trains to Ilfracombe from the GWR for years prior to that. No.6326 heads the 08.02 Wolverhampton Low Level to Ilfracombe on 15th August 1964. The 1924 extension to the footbridge is partially obscured by steam. (E.Wilmshurst)

114. The extensive yard was often full to capacity, but not when photographed in 1969. From 1948 it handled complete wagon loads only, all parcel traffic being transferred to the former GWR station, designated Victoria Road in 1949. A 7½-ton capacity crane was situated at the far end of the yard. (D.J.Aston)

116. The 40-lever "A" or East Box lost its prefix in 1971 and closed on 1st November 1987. The 50ft turntable had been situated on the left of this picture. The table had replaced a 35ft unit in the 1890s. No.31256 is arriving with the 15.05 Sundays-only from Exeter St.Davids on 12th September 1982. Bulk cement and other wagon load traffic continued until 1987. (D.Mitchell)

115. The 07.40 from Paignton is seen on 3rd October 1970, the last day of operation of the branch line to Ilfracombe. The curves were not officially taken out of use until May 1971, prior to which an unsuccessful preservation bid was made. (D.Mitchell)

117. DMU no. P463 waits to return to Exeter at 12.28 on 30th May 1984. The lines converged beyond the bridge at a ground frame. Beyond this stop blocks had been fitted, following the cessation of clay traffic on 31st August 1982. They were removed briefly in 1983 for the passage of a railtour. The other down line had ceased to be used in 1971. (J.Scrace)

118. The first railtour with an HST was on 18th March 1990. Another unusual visit was of the "Taw & Tor Tourer" on 16th September 1990, which was formed of twelve coaches with a class 50 at each end. (R.E.Ruffell)

119. Newspaper traffic ceased in July 1988 and in consequence the 05.50 departure was discontinued. When photographed in April 1992 a "Red Star" parcel service was available, the booking office was still staffed and the station was unusual in having a bicycle hire facility. (V.Mitchell)

120. In August 1980 the remaining track was lifted, except for the platform road, and beyond the station one siding was retained and provided with a loop. The 16.19 seems busy on 26th June 1992. This departure carries a large number of scholars, the line continuing to give a valuable service to the community and to otter watchers. (S.C.Nash)

MP Middleton Press

Easebourne Lane, Midhurst, West Sussex GU29 9AZ
Tel: (0730) 813169 Fax: (0730) 812601

Companion albums in this style for other West of England lines

Branch Lines ...
Branch Lines to Exmouth
Branch Line to Lyme Regis
Branch Line to Lynton
Branch Line to Minehead
Branch Lines to Seaton and Sidmouth
Branch Line to Swanage to 1992
Branch Lines around Weymouth
(Abbotsbury, Easton and The Quay Tramway)

Southern Main Lines ...
Exeter to Barnstaple
Salisbury to Yeovil
Yeovil to Exeter

Country Railway Routes ...
Bath to Evercreech Junction
Bournemouth to Evercreech Junction
Burnham to Evercreech Junction
Yeovil to Dorchester
(including the Bridport Branch)

Write or telephone for the full list of Southern Classics